Introducing the ultimate collection of delicious and nutritious recipes that will tantalize your taste buds and nourish your body! This cookbook is filled with a wide range of healthy and flavorful recipes that are perfect for anyone looking to eat better without sacrificing taste.

Each recipe has been carefully crafted to ensure that it is both delicious and packed with essential nutrients, making it the perfect choice for anyone who wants to improve their health while still enjoying delicious food. From hearty breakfasts and satisfying snacks to mouth-watering mains and delectable desserts, this cookbook has something for everyone.

Whether you're a seasoned cook or a beginner in the kitchen, these recipes are easy to follow and use simple ingredients that can be found at your local grocery store. You'll find everything from plant-based dishes to lean protein-packed meals that are sure to satisfy your cravings and leave you feeling satisfied.

Not only are these recipes healthy and delicious, but they are also beautifully presented with stunning photographs that will inspire you to get creative in the kitchen. You'll learn how to make dishes that are not only good for you but also look and taste amazing.

So, whether you're looking to improve your health, expand your culinary skills, or simply want to try some new and exciting recipes, this cookbook has got you covered. With its mouth-watering recipes and beautiful presentation, it's the perfect addition to any kitchen and is sure to become a go-to resource for anyone who loves good food and good health.

Scallion Egg Wrap

Ingredients:

2 eggs
1 scallion, thinly sliced
1/4 teaspoon salt
1/4 teaspoon black pepper
1 teaspoon vegetable oil or cooking spray
1 large whole wheat tortilla or wrap
1/4 avocado, sliced
1/4 cup shredded cheddar cheese (optional)

Instructions:

In a small bowl, whisk together the eggs, sliced scallion, salt, and black pepper until well combined.

Heat the vegetable oil in a non-stick skillet over medium-high heat.
Pour the egg mixture into the skillet and cook for 2-3 minutes or until the bottom of the egg is set.
Use a spatula to flip the egg over and cook for an additional 1-2 minutes on the other side.
Remove the skillet from the heat and place the tortilla on top of the egg.
Carefully flip the egg and tortilla over so that the tortilla is on the bottom.
Place the sliced avocado and shredded cheddar cheese (if using) on top of the egg.
Use the spatula to carefully fold the sides of the tortilla over the egg, creating a wrap.
Return the skillet to medium heat and cook the wrap for another 1-2 minutes or until the cheese is melted and the tortilla is crispy.
Remove the wrap from the skillet and serve hot.
Enjoy your delicious and satisfying scallion egg wrap!

Vegetable Chow Mein

Ingredients:

8 oz chow mein noodles
2 tbsp vegetable oil
2 cloves garlic, minced
1/2 onion, sliced
1 carrot, julienned
1/2 bell pepper, sliced
1/2 cup sliced mushrooms
1/4 cup soy sauce
2 tbsp hoisin sauce
1 tsp sesame oil
1/4 tsp black pepper

Instructions:

Cook the chow mein noodles according to the package instructions, then drain and set aside.
Heat the vegetable oil in a wok or large skillet over high heat.
Add the minced garlic and sliced onion, and stir-fry for 1-2 minutes or until fragrant.
Add the julienned carrot, sliced bell pepper, and sliced mushrooms, and stir-fry for another 2-3 minutes or until the vegetables are slightly softened.
In a small bowl, whisk together the soy sauce, hoisin sauce, sesame oil, and black pepper.
Add the cooked noodles to the wok or skillet, and pour the sauce over the top.
Use tongs to toss everything together until the noodles are coated in the sauce and the vegetables are evenly distributed.
Serve hot and enjoy your Copycat Panda Express Chow Mein!

Hummus

Ingredients:

1 can (15 oz) of chickpeas, drained and rinsed
1/4 cup tahini
1/4 cup lemon juice
2 garlic cloves, minced
1/2 tsp ground cumin
1/4 tsp paprika
1/4 cup olive oil
Salt to taste
2-3 tbsp water, as needed

Instructions:

In a food processor, combine the chickpeas, tahini, lemon juice, minced garlic, cumin, paprika, and salt.
Process the mixture until it's smooth and creamy, scraping down the sides of the bowl as needed.
While the food processor is still running, slowly pour in the olive oil through the feed tube. This will help emulsify the mixture and make it even creamier.
If the hummus is too thick, add water one tablespoon at a time until it reaches your desired consistency.
Taste the hummus and adjust the seasoning as needed with more salt, lemon juice, or spices.
Serve the hummus with pita bread, veggies, or your favorite dipping vehicle.
Enjoy!

Potatoes With Sea Salt And Rosemary

Ingredients:

2 lbs baby potatoes
2 tbsp olive oil
2 tbsp fresh rosemary, finely chopped
1 tbsp coarse sea salt
Freshly ground black pepper, to taste

Instructions:

Preheat your oven to 400°F (200°C).
Scrub the potatoes and pat them dry with a paper towel.
In a large bowl, toss the potatoes with olive oil, rosemary, sea salt, and black pepper until evenly coated.
Arrange the potatoes in a single layer on a baking sheet lined with parchment paper.
Roast the potatoes in the preheated oven for 30-35 minutes, or until they are crispy on the outside and tender on the inside.
Once the potatoes are done, remove them from the oven and let them cool for a few minutes before serving.
Transfer the potatoes to a serving dish and sprinkle with additional sea salt and black pepper, if desired.
Serve the potatoes as a side dish or snack, garnished with fresh rosemary sprigs. Enjoy!

Shakshuka

Ingredients:

1 large onion, chopped
2 bell peppers (red, yellow, or green), seeded and chopped
4 garlic cloves, minced
1 teaspoon of ground cumin
1 teaspoon of smoked paprika
1/4 teaspoon of cayenne pepper (optional)
1 (28-ounce) can of whole peeled tomatoes, crushed by hand
1/2 cup of vegetable or chicken broth
6-8 large eggs
Salt and pepper, to taste
Fresh parsley or cilantro, chopped, for serving (optional)

Instructions:

Heat olive oil in a large skillet over medium heat.
Add the chopped onion and bell peppers to the skillet, and cook for about 5-7 minutes until softened.
Add minced garlic, ground cumin, smoked paprika, and cayenne pepper (if using) to the skillet, stirring frequently for another 1-2 minutes until fragrant.
Add the crushed tomatoes and vegetable or chicken broth to the skillet, season with salt and pepper to taste, and bring the mixture to a simmer.
Simmer the sauce for about 10-15 minutes until it has thickened and reduced slightly.
Using a spoon, create 6-8 wells in the sauce.
Crack an egg into each well and season the eggs with salt and pepper.
Cover the skillet and cook on medium-low heat for about 5-10 minutes or until the eggs are set to your desired consistency.
Remove the skillet from heat and sprinkle with fresh parsley or cilantro if desired.
Serve the Shakshuka hot with some crusty bread or pita bread to soak up the delicious sauce.
Enjoy your flavorful Mediterranean Shakshuka as a brunch or dinner dish!

Fish Tacos

Ingredients:

1 pound of white fish (such as cod or tilapia), cut into small strips
1/2 cup of all-purpose flour
1/2 teaspoon of cumin
1/2 teaspoon of chili powder
1/2 teaspoon of garlic powder
Salt and pepper to taste
2 tablespoons of vegetable oil
Corn tortillas
Shredded cabbage or lettuce
Sliced avocado
Salsa or pico de gallo
Sour cream
Lime wedges

Instructions:

In a small bowl, whisk together the flour, cumin, chili powder, garlic powder, salt, and pepper.
Dip the fish strips into the flour mixture, coating them evenly.
Heat the vegetable oil in a large skillet over medium-high heat.
Add the coated fish strips to the skillet and cook for 2-3 minutes per side, or until the fish is cooked through and crispy.
Warm the corn tortillas in a separate skillet or in the oven.
To assemble the fish tacos, place a few pieces of cooked fish on each tortilla.
Top with shredded cabbage or lettuce, sliced avocado, salsa or pico de gallo, and a dollop of sour cream.
Squeeze a lime wedge over the top of each taco.
Enjoy your delicious and flavorful Fish Tacos!

Air Fryer Beef & Broccoli

Ingredients:

1 lb. flank steak, sliced thinly against the grain
1 head of broccoli, cut into florets
2 tbsp. soy sauce
2 tbsp. hoisin sauce
1 tbsp. honey
1 tbsp. rice vinegar
1 tbsp. cornstarch
2 cloves garlic, minced
1 tsp. ginger, grated
Salt and pepper to taste
Cooking spray

Instructions:

Preheat your air fryer to 375°F.

In a small bowl, whisk together the soy sauce, hoisin sauce, honey, rice vinegar, cornstarch, garlic, and ginger until well combined.
In a separate bowl, season the sliced flank steak with salt and pepper.
Add the sliced steak to the bowl with the sauce mixture, and toss until the steak is well coated.
Spray the air fryer basket with cooking spray.
Place the coated steak into the air fryer basket, and cook for 8-10 minutes or until the steak is browned and cooked through.
Remove the cooked steak from the air fryer basket, and set it aside on a plate.
Add the broccoli florets to the air fryer basket, and spray them with cooking spray.
Cook the broccoli for 4-5 minutes or until it's crisp-tender.
Add the cooked steak back into the air fryer basket with the cooked broccoli, and toss everything together.
Cook for an additional 2-3 minutes or until the sauce is thickened and the beef and broccoli are heated through.
Serve hot and enjoy!

Seafood Gumbo

Ingredients:

1/2 cup of vegetable oil
1/2 cup of all-purpose flour
1 large onion, chopped
1 green bell pepper, chopped
2 celery stalks, chopped
4 garlic cloves, minced
6 cups of seafood or chicken broth
1 bay leaf
1 teaspoon of dried thyme
1 teaspoon of dried oregano
1/2 teaspoon of cayenne pepper
Salt and black pepper to taste
1 pound of Andouille sausage, sliced
1 pound of medium shrimp, peeled and deveined
1 pound of crabmeat, picked clean
2 tablespoons of Worcestershire sauce
2 tablespoons of file powder
Cooked white rice for serving
Chopped green onions for garnish

Instructions:

In a large Dutch oven, heat the vegetable oil over medium-high heat.
Add the flour to the oil and stir constantly until the mixture turns a deep brown color, about 20-25 minutes.
Add the chopped onion, green pepper, celery, and garlic to the roux and cook for 5-7 minutes, or until the vegetables are softened.
Pour in the seafood or chicken broth and stir well to combine.
Add the bay leaf, thyme, oregano, cayenne pepper, salt, and black pepper to the pot.
Bring the mixture to a boil, then reduce the heat and simmer for 30 minutes, stirring occasionally.
Add the sliced Andouille sausage to the pot and cook for 10-15 minutes.
Add the shrimp and crabmeat to the pot and cook for an additional 5-7 minutes, or until the shrimp are pink and cooked through.
Stir in the Worcestershire sauce and file powder.
Remove the bay leaf from the pot.
Serve the seafood gumbo over cooked white rice, garnished with chopped green onions.
Enjoy your delicious Seafood Gumbo!

Avocado Toast

Avocado toast is a simple and delicious breakfast or snack that has gained popularity in recent years. Here's a recipe for a basic avocado toast:

Ingredients:

1 ripe avocado
2 slices of bread (sourdough, whole grain, or your favorite bread)
1 small garlic clove, minced (optional)
1/2 lemon
Salt and black pepper, to taste
Red pepper flakes (optional)
Olive oil (optional)

Instructions:

Cut the avocado in half, remove the pit, and scoop the flesh into a bowl.
Mash the avocado with a fork or potato masher until it is smooth but still a little chunky.
Add minced garlic (if using), a squeeze of lemon juice, and a pinch of salt and black pepper to the mashed avocado. Mix well to combine.
Toast the bread slices until they are lightly golden brown and crispy.
Spread the mashed avocado evenly on each slice of toast.
Sprinkle some red pepper flakes (if using) and a drizzle of olive oil (if desired) on top of the avocado toast.
Serve immediately and enjoy your tasty and healthy avocado toast!
You can also customize your avocado toast by adding toppings like sliced tomatoes, crumbled feta cheese, or a poached egg

Beef and Broccoli

Ingredients:

1 lb. flank steak, thinly sliced against the grain
1 lb. broccoli florets
2 Tbsp. vegetable oil
3 cloves garlic, minced
1/4 cup soy sauce
2 Tbsp. brown sugar
1 Tbsp. cornstarch
1/4 cup water
1/4 tsp. red pepper flakes (optional)
Cooked rice, for serving

Instructions:

In a mixing bowl, whisk together the soy sauce, brown sugar, cornstarch, water, and red pepper flakes (if using). Set aside.
Heat the vegetable oil in a large skillet or wok over high heat.
Add the sliced flank steak and cook for 2-3 minutes or until browned.
Add the minced garlic and cook for another 30 seconds or until fragrant.
Add the broccoli florets to the skillet and stir-fry everything together for 2-3 minutes or until the broccoli is bright green and slightly tender.
Pour the soy sauce mixture over the beef and broccoli, stirring well to coat everything.
Cook for another 2-3 minutes or until the sauce has thickened and the beef and broccoli are fully coated.
Serve the Beef and Broccoli hot over cooked rice.
Enjoy your delicious Beef and Broccoli!

Spring Rolls

Ingredients:

12-14 spring roll wrappers
2 cups shredded cabbage
1 cup shredded carrot
1 red bell pepper, thinly sliced
1/2 cup sliced scallions
1/4 cup chopped fresh cilantro
1/4 cup chopped fresh mint
1/4 cup chopped fresh basil
1/4 cup tamari or soy sauce
2 tbsp rice vinegar
1 tbsp maple syrup
2 tsp grated ginger
2 cloves garlic, minced
1 tbsp cornstarch
2 tbsp water
Oil for frying

Instructions:

In a large bowl, combine the shredded cabbage, shredded carrot, red bell pepper, scallions, cilantro, mint, and basil.
In a separate bowl, whisk together the tamari, rice vinegar, maple syrup, grated ginger, and minced garlic until well combined.
Pour the tamari mixture over the vegetable mixture and toss until everything is coated evenly.
In a small bowl, whisk together the cornstarch and water to make a slurry.
Lay a spring roll wrapper on a clean surface and place 2-3 tablespoons of the vegetable mixture in the center.
Fold the bottom of the wrapper up over the filling, then fold in the sides and roll the wrapper up tightly. Use the cornstarch slurry to seal the edges of the wrapper.
Repeat with the remaining wrappers and filling.
Heat the oil in a deep skillet or wok over medium-high heat.
Once the oil is hot, add the spring rolls in batches and fry for 2-3 minutes on each side, or until they are golden brown and crispy.
Use a slotted spoon to transfer the spring rolls to a paper towel-lined plate to drain off any excess oil.
Serve the spring rolls hot, with your favorite dipping sauce. Enjoy!

Salmon Burgers

Ingredients:

1 pound of skinless salmon fillet
1/2 cup of panko bread crumbs
1/4 cup of chopped green onions
2 tablespoons of chopped fresh parsley
1 tablespoon of Dijon mustard
1 egg
1 teaspoon of lemon zest
Salt and black pepper to taste
4 burger buns
Lettuce, tomato slices, and mayonnaise
(optional)

Instructions:

Preheat the oven to 375°F.
Cut the salmon into small pieces and put them in a food processor. Pulse until the salmon is coarsely chopped, but not pureed.
In a large bowl, mix together the chopped salmon, bread crumbs, green onions, parsley, Dijon mustard, egg, lemon zest, salt, and pepper.
Divide the salmon mixture into four equal portions and shape each portion into a patty.
Heat a tablespoon of vegetable oil in a large skillet over medium-high heat.
Add the salmon patties to the skillet and cook for 3-4 minutes on each side, or until browned and cooked through.
Transfer the cooked salmon patties to a baking sheet and bake in the oven for 5-7 minutes, or until fully cooked.
Toast the burger buns in the oven or on a grill.
Assemble the burgers by placing a salmon patty on a toasted bun and topping with lettuce, tomato slices, and mayonnaise (if desired).
Enjoy your delicious and healthy Salmon Burgers!

Air Fryer Orange Chicken

Ingredients:

2 boneless, skinless chicken breasts, cut into bite-sized pieces
1/2 cup of cornstarch
1/4 cup of all-purpose flour
1/4 teaspoon of salt
1/4 teaspoon of black pepper
2 eggs, beaten
1/4 cup of orange juice
1/4 cup of honey
2 tablespoons of soy sauce
1 tablespoon of grated ginger
1 tablespoon of grated garlic
1/4 teaspoon of red pepper flakes (optional)
1 tablespoon of cornstarch, mixed with 2 tablespoons of water
Sliced green onions and sesame seeds for garnish (optional)

Instructions:

Preheat your air fryer to 400°F (200°C).
In a mixing bowl, whisk together the cornstarch, flour, salt, and black pepper.
In another mixing bowl, beat the eggs.
Dip each chicken piece into the beaten eggs, then coat them in the cornstarch mixture, pressing the mixture onto the chicken to make sure it sticks.
Lightly spray the air fryer basket with cooking spray.
Arrange the chicken pieces in a single layer in the air fryer basket.
Air fry the chicken for 10-12 minutes or until it is golden brown and crispy, flipping the pieces halfway through the cooking process.
Meanwhile, in a small saucepan, combine the orange juice, honey, soy sauce, grated ginger, grated garlic, and red pepper flakes (if using). Stir well and bring to a simmer over medium heat.
Cook the sauce for 2-3 minutes or until it thickens slightly.
Once the chicken is done, transfer it to a large mixing bowl.
Pour the orange sauce over the chicken and toss to coat evenly.
Place the chicken back in the air fryer basket and air fry for an additional 2-3 minutes or until the sauce is hot and bubbly.
Remove the chicken from the air fryer basket and let it cool for a few minutes.
Garnish with sliced green onions and sesame seeds, if desired.
Serve hot and enjoy your delicious and crispy Air Fryer Orange Chicken!

Soy Garlic Korean Fried Chicken

Ingredients:

2 lbs. chicken wings or drumettes
1/2 cup all-purpose flour
1/2 cup cornstarch
1 tsp. baking powder
Salt and pepper, to taste
Oil, for frying
1/4 cup soy sauce
1/4 cup honey
2 Tbsp. brown sugar
2 Tbsp. rice vinegar
1 Tbsp. sesame oil
4 cloves garlic, minced
1 Tbsp. grated ginger
1-2 green onions, thinly sliced (optional)

Instructions:
In a large mixing bowl, whisk together the flour, cornstarch, baking powder, salt, and pepper. Add the chicken wings or drumettes to the bowl and toss them in the flour mixture until they're evenly coated.
Heat about 1 inch of oil in a large skillet or deep fryer over medium-high heat. Once the oil is hot, carefully add the chicken wings or drumettes to the oil and fry them for about 10-12 minutes or until crispy and cooked through. Drain them on a paper towel-lined plate.
While the chicken is frying, make the sauce. In a small saucepan, whisk together the soy sauce, honey, brown sugar, rice vinegar, sesame oil, garlic, and ginger over medium heat until the sugar has dissolved and the sauce has thickened slightly.
Once the chicken is cooked and drained, toss it in the soy garlic sauce until it's coated evenly.
Serve the Soy Garlic Korean Fried Chicken hot, garnished with thinly sliced green onions, if desired.

Margherita Pizza

Ingredients:

1 batch of pizza dough (store-bought or homemade)
1/2 cup tomato sauce
1/2 teaspoon dried oregano
1/4 teaspoon garlic powder
1/4 teaspoon salt
1/4 teaspoon black pepper
1/2 cup vegan mozzarella cheese, shredded
1 large tomato, thinly sliced
Fresh basil leaves, chopped

Instructions:

Preheat your oven to 425°F (220°C). If you have a pizza stone, place it in the oven while it preheats.
Roll out your pizza dough on a floured surface until it's about 1/4 inch thick. Transfer the dough to a piece of parchment paper.
In a small bowl, mix together the tomato sauce, oregano, garlic powder, salt, and black pepper. Spread the mixture over the pizza dough, leaving a small border around the edges.
Sprinkle the shredded vegan mozzarella cheese over the sauce.
Arrange the tomato slices on top of the cheese.
Transfer the pizza on the parchment paper to the preheated pizza stone or a baking sheet.
Bake the pizza for 10-12 minutes, or until the crust is golden brown and the cheese is melted and bubbly.
Remove the pizza from the oven and sprinkle with fresh chopped basil.
Slice and serve hot.
Enjoy your delicious and vegan-friendly margherita pizza!

Curried Rice

Ingredients:

1 cup white or brown rice
2 cups water
2 tablespoons vegetable oil
1 onion, diced
2 garlic cloves, minced
1 tablespoon curry powder
1/4 teaspoon ground turmeric
1/4 teaspoon ground cumin
1/4 teaspoon ground cinnamon
1/4 teaspoon ground cardamom
1/2 teaspoon salt
1/4 cup raisins
1/4 cup sliced almonds
2 tablespoons chopped fresh parsley or cilantro, for garnish

Instructions:

Rinse the rice in a fine-mesh strainer and drain well.
In a medium-sized saucepan, bring the water to a boil over high heat.
Add the rice to the boiling water and reduce the heat to low. Cover the saucepan with a lid and simmer the rice for 18-20 minutes, or until fully cooked.
While the rice is cooking, heat the vegetable oil in a large skillet over medium heat.
Add the diced onion to the skillet and sauté for 3-4 minutes until softened and translucent.
Add the minced garlic to the skillet and sauté for an additional 30 seconds until fragrant.
Add the curry powder, ground turmeric, ground cumin, ground cinnamon, ground cardamom, and salt to the skillet. Stir well to combine.
Add the cooked rice to the skillet and stir well to coat the rice with the curry mixture.
Add the raisins and sliced almonds to the skillet and stir well to combine.
Garnish the curried rice with chopped fresh parsley or cilantro, if desired.
Serve hot and enjoy!

Lemon Garlic Shrimp

Ingredients:

1 pound of large shrimp, peeled and deveined
3 cloves of garlic, minced
2 tablespoons of olive oil
1/4 cup of dry white wine
1/4 cup of chicken broth
Juice of 1 lemon
2 tablespoons of butter
Salt and black pepper to taste
Chopped fresh parsley for garnish

Instructions:

Heat the olive oil in a large skillet over medium-high heat.
Add the minced garlic and cook for 1-2 minutes, or until fragrant.
Add the shrimp to the skillet and cook for 2-3 minutes on each side, or until pink and cooked through. Remove the shrimp from the skillet and set aside.
Deglaze the skillet with the white wine and chicken broth, scraping up any brown bits from the bottom of the pan.
Add the lemon juice to the skillet and bring the mixture to a simmer.
Add the butter to the skillet and stir until melted and well combined.
Return the shrimp to the skillet and toss with the lemon garlic sauce.
Season with salt and black pepper to taste.
Garnish with chopped fresh parsley and serve immediately.
Enjoy your delicious and flavorful Lemon Garlic Shrimp!

Salmon Patties

Ingredients:

1 pound of skinless salmon fillet
1/4 cup of finely chopped onion
1/4 cup of finely chopped celery
2 tablespoons of mayonnaise
2 tablespoons of Dijon mustard
1 tablespoon of lemon juice
1 teaspoon of Old Bay seasoning
Salt and black pepper to taste
1/2 cup of panko bread crumbs
1/4 cup of chopped fresh parsley
2 tablespoons of olive oil

Instructions:

Cut the salmon into small pieces and put them in a food processor. Pulse until the salmon is coarsely chopped, but not pureed.
In a large bowl, mix together the chopped salmon, chopped onion, chopped celery, mayonnaise, Dijon mustard, lemon juice, Old Bay seasoning, salt, and black pepper.
Add the panko bread crumbs and chopped fresh parsley to the salmon mixture and stir to combine.
Divide the salmon mixture into 8 equal portions and shape each portion into a patty.
Heat the olive oil in a large skillet over medium-high heat.
Add the salmon patties to the skillet and cook for 3-4 minutes on each side, or until browned and cooked through.
Serve hot and enjoy your delicious and flavorful Salmon Patties!
Note: You can also serve the salmon patties with tartar sauce or remoulade sauce for added flavor.

Grilled Chicken Kebab

Ingredients:

1 pound boneless, skinless chicken breasts, cut into 1-inch cubes
1/4 cup olive oil
2 tablespoons fresh lemon juice
2 cloves garlic, minced
1 teaspoon paprika
1 teaspoon ground cumin
1/2 teaspoon salt
1/4 teaspoon black pepper
Wooden or metal skewers
Optional: diced onion, bell pepper, and/or cherry tomatoes for skewering

Instructions:

If using wooden skewers, soak them in water for at least 30 minutes to prevent burning during grilling.
In a small bowl, whisk together the olive oil, lemon juice, garlic, paprika, cumin, salt, and black pepper.
Place the chicken cubes in a large zip-top bag and pour the marinade over the top. Seal the bag and refrigerate for at least 1 hour (or up to 8 hours) to allow the flavors to penetrate the meat.
Preheat a grill to medium-high heat.
If using vegetables, thread them onto skewers along with the marinated chicken cubes.
Grill the chicken kebabs for 10-12 minutes, turning occasionally, until the chicken is cooked through and slightly charred on the outside.
Serve hot, garnished with fresh herbs and a squeeze of lemon juice, if desired. Enjoy!

Baked Feta Pasta

ingredients

2 pints (20 oz) grape tomatoes.
1/2 cup extra-virgin olive oil.
Salt and freshly ground black pepper.
7 oz. block feta cheese (sheep's milk variety), drained.
10 oz. dry pasta (bite size)
5 medium garlic cloves, peeled and halved.
8 oz. ...
1/4 tsp crushed red pepper flakes, or more to taste.

Baked Feta Pasta is an easy and healthy dish that takes only minimal time to prepare. With just a handful of simple ingredients, you can create this delicious meal. To make it, start by preheating your oven to 425 degrees Fahrenheit.

In a large bowl, combine the grape tomatoes, extra-virgin olive oil, salt and pepper. Cut the feta cheese into small cubes and add it to the bowl. Next, cook 10 oz of bite-size pasta according to package instructions until al dente. Once done, drain it and mix it with the tomato mixture in the bowl.

Add garlic cloves, 8 oz of mushrooms (sliced), and 1/4 tsp of crushed red pepper flakes, or to taste. Toss everything together and spread it in a single layer on an oven-safe dish. Bake for 25 minutes until the top is lightly golden brown.

Baked Feta Pasta is now ready to enjoy! Serve with a sprinkling of fresh herbs, extra olive oil, and a side of crusty bread. This healthy pasta dish makes for a great weeknight dinner that is sure to please the whole family. Enjoy!

Chicken Quesadillas

Ingredients

1 pound skinless, boneless chicken breast, diced.
1 (1.27 ounce) packet fajita seasoning.
1 tablespoon vegetable oil.
2 green bell peppers, chopped.
2 red bell peppers, chopped.
1 onion, chopped. ...
10 (10 inch) flour tortillas.
1 (8 ounce) package shredded Cheddar cheese.

Chicken quesadillas make for a healthy and easy dinner for the whole family. To start preparing, dice the boneless chicken breasts and season with fajita seasoning. In a large skillet over medium heat, heat vegetable oil and add in the diced chicken breast, green bell peppers, red bell peppers, and onions. Cook until vegetables are softened and chicken is cooked through. To assemble the quesadillas, place about ¼ cup of cheese onto one side of a tortilla. Top with cooked vegetables and chicken, then add another ¼ cup of cheese to the top. Fold over into a half-moon shape and cook in a skillet on medium-high heat until golden brown. Repeat this process with the remaining tortillas. Serve warm and enjoy!

For a fun variation, try adding black beans to the quesadillas or swapping out Cheddar cheese for Monterey Jack. Using flavorful ingredients like jalapenos, salsa, and guacamole can also liven up this classic dish. Chicken quesadillas make for a healthy and delicious dinner that can be customized to fit the tastes of any family. Enjoy!

Spinach And Feta Pizza

Ingredients

2 large Pizza Bases (see notes)
½ cup Tomato Paste.
½ Brown / Yellow Onion, finely diced.
½ Red Capsicum / Bell Pepper, finely diced.
100g / 3.5 oz Baby Spinach, roughly chopped.
4 White Mushrooms, thinly sliced.
½ cup Feta Cheese, crumbled.
1 ½ cups Shredded Mozzarella Cheese (or more, to taste)

Making delicious spinach and feta pizzas is easy and delicious. To begin, preheat your oven to 200°C / 392°F. Place the pizza bases on a lightly greased baking tray. Spread a thin layer of tomato paste over each base, then scatter the diced onion, capsicum / bell pepper, mushrooms, baby spinach and crumbled feta cheese over the top. Sprinkle with mozzarella cheese (you can add more if desired). Bake for 15-20 minutes or until golden brown and bubbly. Serve hot! Enjoy your delicious spinach and feta pizza!

These delicious spinach and feta pizzas are sure to become a family favorite in no time! The combination of flavors from the vegetables, feta and mozzarella cheese makes for a delicious meal that is sure to please everyone. With just a few simple ingredients, you can easily make delicious pizza recipes at home with ease! No need to order take-out anymore - now you can make delicious pizzas right in your own kitchen. Enjoy!

Sweet and Sour Chicken with Vegetables

Ingredients:

1 lb boneless, skinless chicken breasts, cut into bite-sized pieces
1 green bell pepper, seeded and chopped
1 red bell pepper, seeded and chopped
1 onion, chopped
1 can (8 oz) pineapple chunks in juice
1/4 cup cornstarch
1/4 cup water
1/2 cup white vinegar
1/2 cup ketchup
1/4 cup brown sugar
1 tablespoon soy sauce
1 teaspoon garlic powder
1 teaspoon ginger powder
2 tablespoons vegetable oil
Salt and pepper to taste

Instructions:

In a small bowl, whisk together the cornstarch and water to make a slurry. Set aside.
Drain the pineapple chunks and reserve the juice.
In a large skillet or wok, heat the vegetable oil over medium-high heat.
Add the chicken to the pan and season with salt and pepper. Cook for 6-8 minutes or until golden brown and cooked through.
Remove the chicken from the pan and set aside.
Add the chopped vegetables to the pan and cook for 3-4 minutes or until slightly softened.
In a medium bowl, whisk together the reserved pineapple juice, vinegar, ketchup, brown sugar, soy sauce, garlic powder, and ginger powder.
Pour the sauce over the vegetables and stir to combine.
Bring the sauce to a boil, then reduce the heat to medium-low and let it simmer for 5-7 minutes or until slightly thickened.
Add the chicken and pineapple chunks to the pan and stir to combine.
Pour the cornstarch slurry into the pan and stir to combine.
Cook for an additional 2-3 minutes or until the sauce has thickened and the chicken and vegetables are fully coated.
Serve the Sweet and Sour Chicken over rice or noodles. Enjoy!

Air Fryer Salmon

Ingredients:

2 salmon fillets
1 tablespoon olive oil
1 teaspoon garlic powder
1 teaspoon paprika
1/2 teaspoon salt
1/4 teaspoon black pepper
Lemon wedges, for serving

Instructions:

Preheat your air fryer to 400°F.
Brush the salmon fillets with olive oil on both sides.
In a small bowl, mix together the garlic powder, paprika, salt, and black pepper.
Rub the spice mixture evenly over both sides of the salmon fillets.
Place the seasoned salmon fillets in the air fryer basket.
Cook the salmon in the air fryer for 8-10 minutes, or until it flakes easily with a fork.
Remove the salmon from the air fryer and let it cool for a few minutes.
Serve the salmon with lemon wedges on the side.
Enjoy your delicious and healthy Air Fryer Salmon, with crispy skin and moist flesh. You can also serve it with your favorite sides, such as roasted vegetables or a salad.

Spanish Clams with Chorizo

Ingredients:

1 lb fresh clams, scrubbed and rinsed
2 tablespoons olive oil
2 oz chorizo, sliced
1 small onion, chopped
2 garlic cloves, minced
1/2 teaspoon smoked paprika
1/4 teaspoon cayenne pepper
1/2 cup dry white wine
2 tablespoons chopped fresh parsley
Salt and pepper to taste
Lemon wedges, for serving

Instructions:

In a large skillet, heat the olive oil over medium heat. Add the sliced chorizo and cook for 2-3 minutes, until browned and crispy. Remove the chorizo from the skillet and set aside. Add the chopped onion to the skillet and cook for 2-3 minutes, until softened. Add the minced garlic, smoked paprika, and cayenne pepper, and cook for another minute.

Pour in the white wine and bring the mixture to a simmer. Add the clams to the skillet and cover with a lid. Cook for 3-4 minutes, shaking the skillet occasionally, until the clams have opened.

Discard any clams that have not opened. Return the chorizo to the skillet and stir to combine with the clams and sauce.

Season the dish with salt and pepper to taste. Garnish with chopped fresh parsley and serve with lemon wedges on the side.

Enjoy your Spanish Clams with Chorizo with some crusty bread to soak up the delicious sauce!

Pesto Pasta

Ingredients:

1 pound (450 g) of pasta (such as spaghetti or linguine)
2 cups (80 g) of fresh basil leaves, packed
1/2 cup (75 g) of pine nuts or walnuts
3 cloves of garlic, peeled
1/2 cup (120 ml) of olive oil
1/2 cup (40 g) of nutritional yeast
1 tsp (5 ml) of lemon juice
Salt and black pepper, to taste

Instructions:

Cook the pasta according to the package instructions. Drain and set aside.
While the pasta is cooking, prepare the pesto sauce. In a food processor or blender, combine the basil leaves, pine nuts or walnuts, and garlic. Pulse until everything is chopped.
With the food processor or blender running, slowly drizzle in the olive oil until the mixture becomes a smooth paste.
Add the nutritional yeast and lemon juice to the pesto sauce and pulse until everything is well combined.
Season the pesto sauce with salt and black pepper, to taste.
Toss the cooked pasta with the pesto sauce until everything is well coated.
Serve the vegan pesto pasta hot, with extra nutritional yeast and chopped fresh basil on top, if desired. Enjoy!

Chicken Tacos

Ingredients

¼ cup olive oil.
2 medium yellow onions, finely chopped.
2 bell peppers (any color), finely chopped.
4 cloves garlic, finely chopped.
2 pounds ground chicken (not extra-lean all breast meat)
1 tablespoon paprika.
2 teaspoons ancho chili powder.
1½ teaspoons ground cumin.

Preparing chicken tacos is a healthy and easy dinner option that kids will love. To make them, begin by heating ¼ cup of olive oil in a large skillet over medium-high heat. Add in chopped onions and bell peppers, as well as the minced garlic, stirring everything until it's lightly browned and fragrant. Then, add in the ground chicken, breaking it up with a spoon as you stir. Once the chicken is cooked through, sprinkle in paprika, ancho chili powder and cumin. Stir everything to combine and let it cook for 3-4 minutes until all of the flavors have melded together.
Once done, serve your chicken tacos with tortillas, your favorite toppings and a side dish. Enjoy!

This is an easy yet tasty way to whip up a healthy dinner for the kids! By following these easy steps, you can have a delicious batch of chicken tacos ready in no time. Not only are they healthy and delicious, but your kids will love them too! Try it out today for a quick and tasty dinner option.

Enjoy!

Falafel Burger

Ingredients:

1 can chickpeas, drained and rinsed
1/2 cup chopped onion
3 cloves garlic, minced
1/2 cup chopped fresh parsley
1/4 cup chopped fresh cilantro
1 tsp ground cumin
1 tsp ground coriander
1/2 tsp salt
1/4 tsp black pepper
1/4 cup all-purpose flour
1/4 cup breadcrumbs
4 vegan burger buns
Lettuce, sliced tomato, and sliced red onion for serving
Tahini sauce or vegan mayo for serving

Instructions:

Preheat your oven to 375°F.
In a food processor, pulse the chickpeas, onion, garlic, parsley, cilantro, cumin, coriander, salt, and black pepper until it forms a coarse mixture.
Transfer the mixture to a large mixing bowl and add the flour and breadcrumbs, then mix until everything is well combined.
Using your hands, form the mixture into four equal-sized patties.
Place the patties on a baking sheet lined with parchment paper and bake in the preheated oven for 20-25 minutes, or until golden brown and crispy.
Once the falafel burgers are cooked, remove them from the oven and let them cool for a few minutes.
While the burgers are cooling, lightly toast the burger buns and prepare any desired toppings.
Assemble the burgers by placing a falafel patty on the bottom half of each bun, then adding a layer of lettuce, tomato, and red onion on top.
Drizzle tahini sauce or vegan mayo over the toppings and add the top half of the bun.
Serve the burgers immediately and enjoy your delicious vegan falafel burgers!

Carbonara Spaghetti

Carbonara spaghetti is a delicious recipe for kids to learn how to cook. The ingredients you will need are 100g of pancetta, 50g of pecorino cheese, 50g of parmesan, 3 large eggs, 350g of spaghetti, 2 plump garlic cloves (peeled and left whole), 50g unsalted butter, sea salt, and freshly ground black pepper. To begin cooking this delicious dish, bring a large saucepan of salted water to the boil. Add the spaghetti and cook until al dente (around 8-10 minutes). Meanwhile, fry the pancetta in a dry non-stick frying pan over moderate heat for about 5 minutes until lightly golden. Once cooked, set aside and keep warm. In a small bowl, mix together the pecorino cheese and parmesan with the eggs until you have a creamy sauce. Season well with salt and pepper. When the spaghetti is cooked, drain it, reserving some of the cooking water. Add the spaghetti to the pan with the pancetta and garlic, and stir everything together. Add the butter, stirring until melted. Pour over the egg mixture and toss everything together well with a little of the reserved cooking water - this will help to make it nice and creamy. Serve immediately while still warm. Enjoy!

This delicious carbonara spaghetti dish is sure to be a hit with the whole family. With just a few ingredients and simple steps, your kids can learn to make this delicious dinner in no time! Serve it with a fresh salad on the side for a delicious meal that everyone will love. Enjoy!

Moroccan Lentil Soup

Ingredients:

2 tablespoons olive oil
1 onion, chopped
2 garlic cloves, minced
2 teaspoons ground cumin
1 teaspoon ground coriander
1/2 teaspoon ground cinnamon
1/2 teaspoon ground turmeric
1/4 teaspoon cayenne pepper
2 cups dried red lentils, rinsed and drained
6 cups vegetable broth
1 can (14.5 oz) diced tomatoes, undrained
2 tablespoons tomato paste
1 lemon, juiced
Salt and pepper to taste
Chopped fresh cilantro, for garnish

Instructions:

In a large pot or Dutch oven, heat the olive oil over medium heat. Add the chopped onion and cook for 2-3 minutes, until softened.
Add the minced garlic, cumin, coriander, cinnamon, turmeric, and cayenne pepper to the pot. Cook for 1-2 minutes, stirring constantly, until fragrant.
Add the rinsed lentils, vegetable broth, diced tomatoes (with their juices), and tomato paste to the pot. Bring the mixture to a boil, then reduce the heat to low and simmer for 30-40 minutes, until the lentils are tender.
Remove the pot from the heat and use an immersion blender to puree the soup until smooth (alternatively, you can transfer the soup to a blender and blend in batches, then return to the pot).
Stir in the lemon juice and season the soup with salt and pepper to taste.
Serve the Moroccan Lentil Soup hot, garnished with chopped fresh cilantro.
Enjoy your delicious and nutritious Moroccan Lentil Soup!

Vegan Alfredo Pasta

Ingredients:

12 oz (340 g) of fettuccine pasta
1 1/2 cups (360 ml) of unsweetened almond milk
1/2 cup (120 ml) of vegetable broth
1/2 cup (60 g) of nutritional yeast
3 cloves of garlic, minced
2 tbsp (30 ml) of olive oil
2 tbsp (30 ml) of cornstarch
1 tsp (5 ml) of salt
1/4 tsp (1.25 ml) of black pepper
Fresh parsley or basil, chopped, for garnish

Instructions:

Cook the fettuccine pasta according to the package instructions until al dente. Drain and set aside.
In a small bowl, whisk together the almond milk, vegetable broth, nutritional yeast, cornstarch, salt, and black pepper.
In a large skillet, heat the olive oil over medium heat. Add the minced garlic and sauté for 1-2 minutes, or until fragrant.
Pour the almond milk mixture into the skillet with the garlic and whisk continuously for 3-5 minutes, or until the sauce starts to thicken.
Add the cooked fettuccine to the skillet with the sauce and toss until the pasta is fully coated in the sauce.
Continue to cook the pasta and sauce for 2-3 minutes, or until the sauce has thickened and the pasta is heated through.
Divide the pasta alfredo into bowls and garnish with chopped fresh parsley or basil.
Enjoy your delicious vegan pasta alfredo!

Easy Frittata

Ingredients:

6 large eggs
1/4 cup milk or heavy cream
1/2 teaspoon salt
1/4 teaspoon black pepper
2 tablespoons olive oil
1 small onion, chopped
1 small bell pepper, chopped
1 cup chopped cooked ham, bacon, or sausage
1 cup shredded cheese (cheddar, mozzarella, or your favorite)
Fresh herbs for garnish (optional)

Instructions:

Preheat the oven to 350°F (175°C).

In a large mixing bowl, whisk together the eggs, milk or heavy cream, salt, and black pepper.
Heat the olive oil in a 10-inch oven-safe skillet over medium heat.
Add the chopped onion and bell pepper to the skillet and cook until softened, about 5-7 minutes.
Add the chopped ham, bacon, or sausage to the skillet and cook for another 2-3 minutes until heated through.
Pour the egg mixture into the skillet, and sprinkle the shredded cheese on top.
Gently stir the ingredients with a spatula to distribute the filling evenly in the skillet.
Transfer the skillet to the preheated oven and bake for 15-20 minutes until the frittata is set and the cheese is melted and bubbly.
Remove the skillet from the oven and let it cool for a few minutes.
Use a spatula to slide the frittata onto a large plate. Garnish with fresh herbs, if desired.
Slice the frittata into wedges and serve warm or at room temperature. Enjoy!

Soutzukakia

Ingredients:

1 lb ground beef
1/2 cup breadcrumbs
1 egg
1 onion, grated
2 garlic cloves, minced
1 tablespoon tomato paste
1 tablespoon red wine vinegar
1 tablespoon chopped fresh parsley
1 teaspoon ground cumin
1 teaspoon paprika
Salt and black pepper, to taste
Olive oil, for frying

For the Sauce:

1 can (14.5 oz) diced tomatoes
1 onion, chopped
2 garlic cloves, minced
1/2 cup chicken broth
1 tablespoon tomato paste
1 teaspoon dried oregano
Salt and black pepper, to taste

Instructions:

In a large mixing bowl, combine the ground beef, breadcrumbs, egg, grated onion, minced garlic, tomato paste, red wine vinegar, chopped parsley, ground cumin, paprika, salt, and black pepper. Mix well until all the ingredients are evenly combined.
Shape the mixture into oval-shaped meatballs, about 2 inches in length.
Heat the olive oil in a large skillet over medium heat. When the oil is hot, add the meatballs to the skillet and cook for 8-10 minutes, turning occasionally, until browned on all sides. Remove the meatballs from the skillet and set aside.
In the same skillet, add the chopped onion and minced garlic. Cook for 2-3 minutes, stirring constantly, until softened.
Pour the diced tomatoes (with their juice), chicken broth, tomato paste, dried oregano, salt, and black pepper into the skillet. Stir to combine.
Return the meatballs to the skillet and spoon the tomato sauce over them.
Reduce the heat to low and cover the skillet with a lid. Simmer for 20-25 minutes, until the meatballs are cooked through and tender.
Serve the Soutzoukakia hot, with the tomato sauce spooned over them. You can serve it with rice or crusty bread on the side.
Enjoy your delicious and fragrant Soutzoukakia!

Air Fryer Chicken Wings

Ingredients:

2 pounds of chicken wings, tips removed and drumettes and flats separated
1 tablespoon of baking powder
1 teaspoon of garlic powder
1 teaspoon of onion powder
1 teaspoon of smoked paprika
Salt and black pepper to taste
Cooking spray
Your favorite wing sauce, for serving (optional)

Instructions:

Preheat your air fryer to 400°F (200°C).
In a small mixing bowl, whisk together the baking powder, garlic powder, onion powder, smoked paprika, salt, and black pepper.
Pat the chicken wings dry with paper towels, then add them to a large mixing bowl.
Sprinkle the seasoning mixture over the chicken wings, then toss gently to coat them evenly.
Lightly spray the air fryer basket with cooking spray.
Arrange the chicken wings in a single layer in the air fryer basket.
Air fry the chicken wings for 20-25 minutes, flipping them halfway through the cooking process, until they are golden brown and crispy.
Once done, remove the chicken wings from the air fryer basket and let them rest for a few minutes.
If desired, toss the chicken wings in your favorite wing sauce.
Serve the chicken wings hot with celery sticks, carrot sticks, and blue cheese or ranch dressing on the side for dipping.
Enjoy your delicious and crispy Air Fryer Chicken Wings!

Beer Battered Fish

Ingredients:

1 pound white fish fillets (such as cod or haddock)
1 cup all-purpose flour
1 teaspoon baking powder
1/2 teaspoon salt
1/2 teaspoon black pepper
1/2 teaspoon paprika
1/2 cup beer (such as lager or pilsner)
1/4 cup milk
Vegetable oil, for frying

Instructions:

In a large bowl, whisk together the flour, baking powder, salt, black pepper, and paprika. Slowly pour in the beer and milk, whisking constantly until the batter is smooth and lump-free.
Place the fish fillets in the batter and coat them evenly, using a fork to flip and coat each piece.
In a large skillet or a deep fryer, heat the vegetable oil over medium-high heat until it reaches 375°F.
Shake off any excess batter from the fish fillets and carefully place them in the hot oil.
Fry the fish fillets for 4-5 minutes, or until they are golden brown and crispy on the outside.
Use a slotted spoon to transfer the fried fish fillets to a paper towel-lined plate to drain off any excess oil.
Repeat the frying process with the remaining fish fillets, adjusting the heat as needed to maintain the oil temperature.
Serve the beer battered fish hot, with lemon wedges and your favorite dipping sauce on the side.
Enjoy your crispy and flavorful Beer Battered Fish, with a crunchy coating that complements the juicy and flaky fish meat.

Lemon Mushroom Chicken

Ingredients:

4 chicken breasts (about 3/4 pound total)
1 1/2 tbsp unsalted butter, divided
8 oz cremini mushrooms, sliced
1/4 tsp salt
1/2 cup dry sherry
1/4 cup lemon juice
1/2 cup heavy cream
2 1/2 cups baby spinach

Instructions:

Season the chicken breasts with salt and pepper.

In a large pan, heat 1 tbsp of butter over medium heat. Add the chicken breasts and cook for about 4-5 minutes on each side, or until golden brown and fully cooked. Remove the chicken from the pan and set aside.

In the same pan, add the remaining butter and sliced mushrooms. Cook the mushrooms for about 4-5 minutes, or until they are tender and lightly browned.

Add the sherry to the pan and use a wooden spoon to scrape the bottom of the pan to release any browned bits. Cook the sherry for about 2 minutes, or until it has reduced by half.

Add the lemon juice and heavy cream to the pan and stir to combine. Cook the sauce for about 2-3 minutes, or until it has thickened slightly.

Return the chicken breasts to the pan and add the baby spinach. Stir to combine and cook for about 2 minutes, or until the spinach has wilted.

Serve the chicken with the lemon mushroom sauce on top. Enjoy!

Air Fryer Sweet Potato Hash

Ingredients:

2 medium sweet potatoes, peeled and diced into small cubes
1 red bell pepper, seeded and diced
1 yellow onion, diced
2 cloves of garlic, minced
2 tablespoons of olive oil
1 teaspoon of smoked paprika
1/2 teaspoon of ground cumin
Salt and pepper, to taste
Fresh parsley, chopped (optional)

Instructions:

In a mixing bowl, toss the diced sweet potatoes, red bell pepper, yellow onion, minced garlic, olive oil, smoked paprika, ground cumin, salt, and pepper until well coated.
Preheat your air fryer to 375°F (190°C).
Lightly spray the air fryer basket with cooking spray.
Spread the sweet potato mixture out in a single layer in the air fryer basket.
Air fry the sweet potato hash for 15-20 minutes, shaking the basket halfway through, until the sweet potatoes are tender and lightly browned.
Once done, remove the sweet potato hash from the air fryer basket and transfer it to a serving plate.
Garnish with chopped fresh parsley (if desired) and serve the Air Fryer Sweet Potato Hash warm as a delicious side dish or breakfast dish. Enjoy!
Note: You can also add diced bacon or sausage to the sweet potato hash for added flavor and protein.

Homemade Naan

Ingredients:

2 cups all-purpose flour
1/2 teaspoon salt
1/2 teaspoon sugar
1/2 teaspoon baking powder
1/4 teaspoon baking soda
3/4 cup warm milk
1/4 cup plain yogurt
1 egg
2 tablespoons melted butter

Instructions:

In a large bowl, whisk together the flour, salt, sugar, baking powder, and baking soda.

In a separate bowl, whisk together the warm milk, plain yogurt, egg, and melted butter.

Gradually add the wet ingredients to the dry ingredients, stirring until a soft, sticky dough forms.

Knead the dough on a floured surface for about 5 minutes, until smooth and elastic.

Place the dough in a greased bowl, cover with a damp cloth, and let it rest for about 30 minutes.

Preheat a skillet or griddle over medium-high heat.

Divide the dough into 6-8 equal parts and roll each part into a thin, oval-shaped disc.

Place the rolled-out naan on the hot skillet or griddle and cook for 1-2 minutes on each side, until golden brown and puffed up.

Brush the cooked naan with melted butter and serve hot.

Mediterranean Zucchini Boats

Ingredients:

4 medium zucchinis
1/2 cup cooked quinoa
1/2 cup crumbled feta cheese
1/2 cup cherry tomatoes, halved
1/4 cup chopped kalamata olives
1/4 cup chopped fresh parsley
2 tablespoons olive oil
2 cloves garlic, minced
1/2 teaspoon dried oregano
Salt and black pepper, to taste
Lemon wedges, for serving (optional)

Instructions:

Preheat the oven to 400°F (200°C).
Cut the zucchinis in half lengthwise and scoop out the seeds with a spoon to create a hollow space in the center of each half. Place the zucchini halves in a baking dish.
In a bowl, combine the cooked quinoa, feta cheese, cherry tomatoes, kalamata olives, and parsley.
In a small saucepan, heat the olive oil over medium heat. Add the minced garlic and dried oregano and cook for 1 to 2 minutes, stirring constantly, until fragrant.
Pour the garlic and oregano mixture over the quinoa mixture and stir to combine. Season with salt and black pepper to taste.
Spoon the quinoa mixture into the hollowed-out zucchini halves, filling them generously.
Cover the baking dish with foil and bake for 25 to 30 minutes, or until the zucchinis are tender and the filling is hot and bubbly.
Remove from the oven and let cool for a few minutes before serving.
Serve the zucchini boats with lemon wedges on the side, if desired.
Enjoy your delicious Mediterranean Zucchini Boats!

Pineapple Baked Salmon

Ingredients:

4 salmon fillets
1 cup fresh pineapple chunks
1/4 cup soy sauce
1/4 cup honey
2 tablespoons rice vinegar
1 tablespoon minced garlic
1 tablespoon minced ginger
1/4 teaspoon black pepper
2 tablespoons chopped green onions (optional)

Instructions:

Preheat your oven to 375°F.
In a small mixing bowl, whisk together the soy sauce, honey, rice vinegar, minced garlic, minced ginger, and black pepper.
Place the salmon fillets in a baking dish that has been lightly sprayed with cooking spray.
Pour the soy sauce mixture over the salmon fillets.
Add the fresh pineapple chunks to the baking dish, distributing them evenly around the salmon fillets.
Cover the baking dish with foil and bake in the preheated oven for 15-20 minutes, or until the salmon is cooked through and flakes easily with a fork.
Remove the foil and broil the salmon for an additional 1-2 minutes, or until the top is browned and caramelized.
Garnish with chopped green onions, if desired, and serve hot.
Enjoy your delicious Pineapple Baked Salmon!

Air Fryer Tuscan Stuffed Mushrooms

Ingredients:

12 large mushrooms
1/2 cup bread crumbs
1/4 cup grated Parmesan cheese
1/4 cup chopped fresh parsley
1/4 cup chopped sun-dried tomatoes
2 cloves garlic, minced
2 tbsp olive oil
Salt and pepper to taste

Instructions:

Preheat your air fryer to 375°F.
Wash the mushrooms and remove the stems. Set the mushroom caps aside.
In a mixing bowl, combine the bread crumbs, grated Parmesan cheese, chopped parsley, chopped sun-dried tomatoes, minced garlic, olive oil, and salt and pepper to taste.
Mix the ingredients together until they are evenly combined.
Stuff each mushroom cap with the filling mixture, pressing down gently to pack it in.
Place the stuffed mushrooms in the air fryer basket and cook for 8-10 minutes, or until the mushrooms are tender and the filling is lightly browned and crispy.
Serve the stuffed mushrooms immediately, garnished with extra Parmesan cheese and fresh parsley if desired.
Enjoy your delicious Air Fryer Tuscan Stuffed Mushrooms!

Air Fryer Crispy Chicken Sandwich

Ingredients:

2 boneless, skinless chicken breasts
1/2 cup all-purpose flour
1 teaspoon salt
1 teaspoon paprika
1/2 teaspoon garlic powder
1/2 teaspoon onion powder
1/4 teaspoon black pepper
2 eggs
1 tablespoon water
1 cup panko bread crumbs
Cooking spray
4 brioche buns
4 lettuce leaves
4 slices of tomato
4 slices of cheddar cheese
Mayo
Ketchup
Pickles (optional)

Instructions:

Preheat your air fryer to 400°F (200°C).
In a shallow dish, mix together the flour, salt, paprika, garlic powder, onion powder, and black pepper.
In a separate shallow dish, whisk together the eggs and water.
In another shallow dish, place the panko bread crumbs.
Slice each chicken breast in half horizontally to make 4 thin chicken cutlets.
Coat each chicken cutlet in the flour mixture, shaking off any excess.
Dip the chicken cutlets into the egg mixture, allowing any excess to drip off.
Coat the chicken cutlets in the panko bread crumbs, pressing the crumbs onto the chicken to make sure they stick.
Place the chicken cutlets in a single layer in the air fryer basket. Spray them lightly with cooking spray.
Air fry the chicken cutlets for 10-12 minutes, flipping them halfway through cooking, until they are golden brown and crispy.
While the chicken is cooking, lightly toast the brioche buns.
Assemble the sandwiches by spreading mayo and ketchup on the bottom of the buns. Add a lettuce leaf and a slice of tomato to each bun.
Place the cooked chicken cutlets on top of the tomato slices. Add a slice of cheddar cheese and pickles, if desired.
Serve the sandwiches immediately and enjoy!

Pasta alla Norma

Ingredients:

1 lb spaghetti
1 large eggplant, diced
2 cloves garlic, minced
1 can (28 oz) whole peeled tomatoes, crushed by hand
1/4 teaspoon red pepper flakes
Salt and pepper to taste
1/4 cup chopped fresh basil
1/2 cup grated ricotta salata cheese
Extra-virgin olive oil

Instructions:

Bring a large pot of salted water to a boil. Add the spaghetti and cook according to package instructions until al dente.

While the spaghetti cooks, heat a large skillet over medium-high heat. Add enough olive oil to coat the bottom of the pan.
Add the diced eggplant to the skillet and cook for about 8-10 minutes, or until the eggplant is golden brown and tender.
Add the minced garlic and red pepper flakes to the skillet and cook for another minute, or until fragrant.
Add the crushed tomatoes to the skillet and season with salt and pepper to taste.
Simmer the sauce for about 10-15 minutes, or until it has thickened slightly.
Drain the cooked spaghetti and add it to the skillet with the tomato sauce. Toss to combine.
Remove the skillet from the heat and stir in the chopped basil.
Divide the pasta among four bowls and sprinkle each serving with grated ricotta salata cheese.
Enjoy your delicious Pasta alla Norma!

Bolognese Pasta

Ingredients:

1 pound of spaghetti or pasta of your choice
1 large onion, chopped
3 garlic cloves, minced
2 carrots, finely chopped
2 celery stalks, finely chopped
1 red bell pepper, chopped
1 can (28 ounces) of crushed tomatoes
1 can (15 ounces) of tomato sauce
1 tablespoon of tomato paste
1 teaspoon of dried oregano
1 teaspoon of dried basil
1 teaspoon of dried thyme
1 teaspoon of salt
1/2 teaspoon of black pepper
2 tablespoons of olive oil
1/4 cup of chopped fresh parsley
Vegan Parmesan cheese for serving (optional)

Instructions:

Cook the pasta according to package instructions until al dente. Drain the pasta and set it aside.
In a large pot or Dutch oven, heat the olive oil over medium-high heat. Add the onion and sauté for 3-4 minutes, or until the onion is translucent.
Add the garlic, carrots, celery, and red bell pepper to the pot. Cook for 5-7 minutes or until the vegetables are tender.
Add the crushed tomatoes, tomato sauce, tomato paste, dried oregano, dried basil, dried thyme, salt, and black peper to the pot. Stir well to combine.
Bring the sauce to a boil, then reduce the heat to low and let it simmer for 20-25 minutes, stirring occasionally.
Once the sauce has thickened and the vegetables are tender, add the chopped fresh parsley and stir well.
Serve the sauce over the cooked pasta and top with vegan Parmesan cheese (if using). Enjoy your delicious vegan bolognese pasta!

Risotto

Ingredients:

1 1/2 cups Arborio or Carnaroli rice
4 cups chicken or vegetable broth
1/2 cup dry white wine
1/4 cup unsalted butter
1/2 cup grated Parmesan cheese
1 onion, finely chopped
2 garlic cloves, minced
2 tablespoons olive oil
Salt and freshly ground black pepper
Optional ingredients: mushrooms, asparagus, peas, shrimp, chicken, or any other vegetables or proteins you'd like to add

Instructions:

In a large saucepan, heat the broth over medium heat until it's simmering.
In a separate large pot, heat the olive oil over medium heat. Add the chopped onion and minced garlic and sauté until the onion is translucent, about 5 minutes.
Add the Arborio rice to the pot and stir to coat the rice in the oil, onion, and garlic mixture.
Add the white wine and stir continuously until it has been absorbed by the rice.
Begin adding the simmering broth to the pot, one cup at a time, stirring constantly until each cup of broth has been absorbed by the rice before adding the next.
Continue adding broth and stirring until the rice is tender and creamy. This process should take about 20-25 minutes.
When the rice is done, stir in the grated Parmesan cheese and season with salt and pepper to taste.
Serve immediately and enjoy!

Tomato Soup

Ingredients:

2 tablespoons olive oil
1 large onion, chopped
3 garlic cloves, minced
2 cans of whole peeled tomatoes
2 cups of vegetable broth
1/4 cup of fresh basil leaves, chopped
1/2 cup of heavy cream (optional)
Salt and pepper to taste
Croutons or bread for serving (optional)

Instructions:

In a large pot or Dutch oven, heat the olive oil over medium heat.
Add the onion and garlic and cook for 5-7 minutes until softened and translucent.
Add the cans of whole peeled tomatoes (with their juice) and stir to combine.
Add the vegetable broth and bring the mixture to a simmer.
Cook for 15-20 minutes until the tomatoes have broken down and the flavors have melded together.
Add the chopped basil leaves and stir to combine.
Using an immersion blender or working in batches with a regular blender, puree the soup until smooth.
Return the soup to the pot and add the heavy cream (if using). Stir to combine.
Season with salt and pepper to taste.
Serve the soup hot with croutons or bread for dipping, if desired.
Enjoy your tomato basil soup! It's a comforting and classic dish that's perfect for any time of year.

Cheesy Broccoli Pasta

Ingredients
½ cup butter.
1 onion, chopped. Fresh Onions.
1 (16 ounce) package frozen chopped broccoli.
4 (14.5 ounce) cans chicken broth.
1 (1 pound) loaf processed cheese food, cubed.
2 cups milk.
1 tablespoon garlic powder.
⅔ cup cornstarch.

This delicious cheesy broccoli pasta is a sure hit for kids and adults alike! With just a few simple steps, anyone can make this delicious dish in no time.

First, melt the butter in a large pot over medium heat. Add the chopped onion and cook until softened, about 5 minutes. Next, add the frozen chopped broccoli and chicken broth and bring to a boil. Reduce the heat, cover, and simmer for 15 minutes.

Once done, add the cubed cheese food, milk, garlic powder and cornstarch to the pot. Give it all a good stir then cover and cook for about 10 more minutes or until the sauce has thickened. Serve hot with your favorite sides!

This cheesy broccoli pasta is delicious and easy to make, making it an ideal recipe for kids. If you're looking for a delicious and nutritious dish that your whole family can enjoy, this is the perfect choice! So what are you waiting for? Try out this delicious cheesy broccoli pasta today!

Enjoy

Greek Moussaka

Ingredients:

2 large eggplants, sliced lengthwise
1 pound ground beef
1 onion, chopped
2 cloves garlic, minced
2 tablespoons tomato paste
1/2 cup red wine
1 can (14.5 oz) diced tomatoes
1 teaspoon dried oregano
1/4 teaspoon ground cinnamon
Salt and black pepper, to taste
3 tablespoons butter
3 tablespoons all-purpose flour
2 cups milk
1/4 teaspoon ground nutmeg
1/2 cup grated Parmesan cheese
1 egg, beaten

Instructions:

Preheat the oven to 375°F (190°C).
Arrange the eggplant slices on a baking sheet and brush both sides with olive oil. Bake for 20 to 25 minutes, or until tender and lightly browned. Set aside.
In a large skillet, cook the ground beef over medium heat until browned. Drain the excess fat.
Add the chopped onion and minced garlic to the skillet and cook until the onion is soft and translucent.
Stir in the tomato paste, red wine, diced tomatoes, oregano, cinnamon, salt, and black pepper.
Bring to a simmer and cook for 10 to 15 minutes, or until the sauce is thick and flavorful.
In a small saucepan, melt the butter over medium heat. Whisk in the flour and cook for 1 to 2 minutes, stirring constantly, until the mixture is smooth and bubbly.
Gradually whisk in the milk and cook for 5 to 7 minutes, or until the sauce is thick and creamy.
Stir in the nutmeg and grated Parmesan cheese.
In a 9x13 inch baking dish, arrange half of the eggplant slices in a single layer. Spoon the meat sauce over the eggplant, spreading it evenly. Arrange the remaining eggplant slices on top of the meat sauce.
Whisk the beaten egg into the Parmesan cheese sauce and pour it over the top of the eggplant.
Bake for 30 to 35 minutes, or until the top is golden and the moussaka is hot and bubbly.
Let the moussaka cool for a few minutes before serving.
Enjoy your delicious Greek Moussaka!

Baked Potato Bar

Ingredients

5 pounds baked potatoes.
3-5 pounds pulled pork cooked.
2 cups sharp cheddar cheese shredded.
1/2 pound bacon cooked & crumbled.
1 cup sour cream.
1/2 cup chives chopped.
2 cups broccoli cooked.
1 bottle bbq sauce.

A baked potato bar is an easy and healthy dinner option for kids, and it's simple to prepare. Start by baking five pounds of potatoes according to the instructions on the package. While they're cooking, pre-cook three to five pounds of pulled pork as well as one-half pound of bacon. Once the potatoes are done, split them open and sprinkle two cups of shredded sharp cheddar cheese over the top. Then, add the cooked pulled pork, crumbled bacon, one cup of sour cream, half a cup of chopped chives and two cups of cooked broccoli. Finally, make sure to provide some BBQ sauce for everyone to enjoy. With minimal effort, you can create a delicious and nutritious baked potato bar that all the kids will love! Enjoy!

Crispy Baked Falafel

Here's a recipe for crispy baked falafel:

Ingredients:

2 cups cooked chickpeas, drained and rinsed
1/2 onion, chopped
3 cloves garlic, minced
1/4 cup chopped fresh parsley
1/4 cup chopped fresh cilantro
1 teaspoon ground cumin
1 teaspoon ground coriander
1/2 teaspoon paprika
1/4 teaspoon cayenne pepper
1 teaspoon salt
1/4 teaspoon black pepper
1/4 cup all-purpose flour
1 teaspoon baking powder
2 tablespoons olive oil

Instructions:

Preheat the oven to 375°F (190°C) and line a baking sheet with parchment paper.
In a food processor, pulse the chickpeas, onion, garlic, parsley, cilantro, cumin, coriander, paprika, cayenne pepper, salt, and black pepper until the mixture is coarse and crumbly.
Add the flour and baking powder to the food processor and pulse until the mixture forms a dough.
Form the dough into 2-inch balls and flatten slightly to form patties.
Place the patties on the prepared baking sheet and brush each one with olive oil.
Bake for 20-25 minutes, or until the falafel is crispy and golden brown.
Serve the falafel with pita bread, hummus, and your favorite veggies. Enjoy!

Mushroom Burger

Here's a recipe for a delicious mushroom burger:

Ingredients:

4 portobello mushroom caps
1/4 cup balsamic vinegar
2 tablespoons olive oil
1 teaspoon dried thyme
1/2 teaspoon garlic powder
Salt and black pepper
4 burger buns
Toppings of your choice
(lettuce, tomato, onion, etc.)

Instructions:

Preheat your grill or grill pan to medium-high heat.
Clean the portobello mushrooms and remove the stems. Use a spoon to gently scrape out the gills and discard them.
In a small bowl, whisk together the balsamic vinegar, olive oil, thyme, garlic powder, salt, and pepper.
Brush the marinade over both sides of the mushroom caps, making sure they are fully coated.
Place the mushrooms on the grill and cook for 4-5 minutes on each side, or until they are tender and juicy.
While the mushrooms are cooking, toast your burger buns on the grill.
Assemble your burgers by placing the cooked mushrooms on the toasted buns and adding your desired toppings.
Serve immediately and enjoy your delicious mushroom burger!

Sesame-Ginger Beef

Ingredients:

1 pound flank steak, thinly sliced against the grain
1/4 cup soy sauce
2 tablespoons rice vinegar
2 tablespoons honey
2 tablespoons sesame oil
2 cloves garlic, minced
1 tablespoon fresh ginger, minced
1/4 teaspoon red pepper flakes (optional)
2 tablespoons vegetable oil
1 red bell pepper, sliced
1 green bell pepper, sliced
4 green onions, sliced
2 tablespoons sesame seeds, toasted

Directions:

In a large bowl, whisk together the soy sauce, rice vinegar, honey, sesame oil, garlic, ginger, and red pepper flakes (if using). Add the sliced beef and toss to coat. Let marinate for at least 15 minutes, or up to 1 hour.
Heat the vegetable oil in a large skillet over medium-high heat. Add the bell peppers and cook until slightly softened, about 2-3 minutes. Add the marinated beef to the skillet and cook, stirring occasionally, until browned and cooked through, about 5-7 minutes. Stir in the sliced green onions and cook for another 1-2 minutes. Sprinkle with toasted sesame seeds and serve immediately over rice or noodles.
Enjoy your Sesame-Ginger Beef!

Cauliflower Rice

Here's how to make cauliflower rice:

Ingredients:

1 head of cauliflower
1 tablespoon olive oil
Salt and pepper to taste

- Instructions:
-
- Wash and dry the cauliflower head.
- Cut off the florets from the stem and discard the stem.
- Place the cauliflower florets in a food processor and pulse until they resemble rice.
- Heat the olive oil in a large skillet over medium-high heat.
- Add the cauliflower rice to the skillet and stir to combine with the oil.
- Season with salt and pepper to taste.
- Cook for 5-7 minutes, stirring occasionally, until the cauliflower rice is tender and slightly golden brown.
- Remove from heat and use as a base for your grain-free grain bowl.

Chicken Noodle Casserole

Ingredients
12 oz. wide egg noodles.
10.5-oz. cans cream of chicken soup.
1 c. whole milk.
1 c. shredded sharp cheddar cheese.
1 tsp. ground black pepper.
1/2 tsp. kosher salt.
3 c. cooked, shredded chicken (from 1 rotisserie chicken)
1/2. small yellow onion, finely chopped.

Making a chicken noodle casserole is an easy and healthy dinner option for kids. To begin, preheat your oven to 400 degrees Fahrenheit. In a large pot over medium heat, cook the egg noodles according to package directions. Drain the cooked noodles and set aside.
In a medium-sized bowl, combine the cream of chicken soup, milk, shredded cheese, ground black pepper and kosher salt. Stir until the ingredients are completely blended.
In a 9-by-13-inch baking dish, spread the cooked egg noodles. Top with the shredded chicken and onion pieces. Pour the cream of chicken mixture over the noodles and chicken, spreading evenly to ensure everything is coated.
Bake for 25 minutes until the cheese is melted and bubbly. Let cool for about 10 minutes before serving. Enjoy!
This chicken noodle casserole provides a comforting, delicious and healthy dinner option for kids. It's quick to prepare, full of flavor and sure to please everyone at the table.

I want to take a moment to express my heartfelt gratitude for your recent purchase of my recipe book. As a passionate food lover, nothing makes me happier than sharing my favorite recipes with others. Your decision to invest in my book not only supports my dream, but also shows your commitment to expanding your culinary horizons.

I sincerely hope that the recipes in the book will inspire you to try new things and add some excitement to your meals.

Thank you again for your support and for being a part of this journey with me. I hope my book will bring you many happy and delicious moments in the kitchen.

www.ingramcontent.com/pod-product-compliance
Lightning Source LLC
Chambersburg PA
CBHW081236080526
44587CB00022B/3965